T0196917

A GUIDE TO
GRIEVING

"THE MISUNDERSTANDING OF GRIEF"

DOCTOR M. E. LYONS

authorHOUSE®

AuthorHouse™
1663 Liberty Drive
Bloomington, IN 47403
www.authorhouse.com
Phone: 1 (800) 839-8640

Published by AuthorHouse 08/31/2016

ISBN: 978-1-5246-2687-7 (sc)
ISBN: 978-1-5246-2686-0 (e)

Print information available on the last page.

This book is printed on acid-free paper.

TABLE OF CONTENTS

Introduction

The late Doctor C.A.W. Clark of the historic Good Street Missionary Baptist Church in Dallas, Texas once asked of my Pastor, the Reverend Doctor S.C. Nash, Sr. in a homily once preached at a three o'clock program to write a book on death and grieving upon the season of separation after his son passed away. I am in full agreement that there should be something that all of us could relate to. To that end, we pen this book. We offer this book as an honor yielded to the late great Doctor C.A.W. Clark's request on that Sunday afternoon as he Preached that pointed Homily at the Mount Tabor Missionary Baptist Church in Dallas, Texas.

Hurtful/Insensitive Sympathy Cliché's

You will get over it!
Don't cry!
I have been where you
have been before!
God wanted to pick his
most beautiful flower!
Call me if you need me!
I have sat where you
are sitting now!
I am sorry for your loss!
I hurt as you hurt!
I know how you feel!
It will get better!

It will get easier!
How do you feel?
How are you doing?
Don't cry too long!
I will always be
here for you!
Are you alright?
We all have to go this way!
Do you need anything?
What happened?
Had she/he been sick?
You sure did put
them away nice!

These few clichés are things that are said and are insensitive, upsetting and mostly unbiblical. We should learn to not say things that will tear down a loved one or friend; but to build up by uttering things that will empower, enable, and endue those experiencing their seasons of separation with strength from on high! I have begun trying to practice perfecting the Ministry of silence when it comes to visiting those who are at this place in life; sometimes the best thing to say to someone experiencing their season of separation is to sometimes; say nothing at all!

MY STORY-
"I'LL BE MOVING ON
THE FIRST OF JANUARY"

My Father the Reverend L. Charles "Chuck" E. Lyons was a unique man! His hands large and bulky, his way of being a disciplinarian, and his model of family first. I loved and love my Father for those reasons and many more. I shall never forget the day my life was changed forever. It was on the twenty-third day of December. A friend and brother of mine Pastor M. Clay Price from Rowlett, Texas had some work for his business to be conducted an hour or so from where I live in Lufkin and

he decided to ask me to ride with him for the sake of company and fellowship. So we went to the place he was designated to go and my phone began to ring and who was it? You guessed it; my Father on the other end and he was talking a bit rushed this time; and said to me: "Myron I am finally going to do what you wanted me to do and go into a nursing home and get the care that I need; due to the fact that your Mother cannot do it and I will be checking in on the first of January; I only have three minutes' left on this phone so I will call you back later." We hung up and I shared with my friend I am glad that he will finally have someone to help him around the clock and we continued our conversation and he dropped me back off at home and about thirty to forty minutes after he dropped me off my phone rang again from my Father's number; I answered and my Mother was crying and saying: "Myron, I think he is gone; I think your Father is dead." I said Mama, what? I screamed (many times I believe) and threw my phone; because I had just spoken with him and everything was alright and being four hours away was even more excruciating. My wife picked up the phone and instructed her to call 911 and while they were talking…his three minutes were up and the call was terminated. Wow; really in the middle of such an important call? Needless to say, I began to go through some of the stages of grief at a very high rate of speed. I was angry because I had stood by the beds of many of our parishioners and witnessed them draw their last breaths. I had been summoned by loved ones to be there in their hours of need and now I cannot even get to my own Father. If only I could have made it; surely I could have prayed him back to life; or been there to hear him say something that I needed to know or do! Now he is gone without notice; without warning. You could probably imagine: I was hurt to *the core. This is my story, and I want someone else to be helped by this story and this book to know that…things happen the way that they do for a REASON!*

My Daddy: The late Reverend L.C.E. Lyons
February 21, 1936-December 23, 2013
The Reverend Doctor M.E. Lyons

"I WANT MY DADDY!"

My sister Anncee was one of a kind and many times we spent arguing and fighting; but it was all in love. We had times whereas we did not get along; but the truth is, no one better do anything to either of us because there was going to be a major problem. She was my protector; and I was her protector. It was on the 25th day of August, 2016. This day changed my life forever. My baby Sister snuck away without saying farewell. I remember as if it were yesterday, there were several calls around 5:30-6 a.m. I finally rolled over and picked up the phone and it was my brother in-law Will Thornton. He said Myron I have some bad news. I knew then what the following words would be and I immediately fell into tears and wept bitterly. My heart was in pieces and was completely broken. Not the person who we made mud pies together, played house and the doors on our rooms across from each other in our parents' house were our apartments, not the one who was my first Church secretary in our backyard. This is the only Sister I knew growing up. Certainly this could not be true. Well, needless to say; my wife grabbed the phone to figure out what was going on and I lost it! I was in total denial and crushed. After all, I had recently celebrated my 40th birthday a week ago and I had the chance to speak to her since she could not make my party. We spoke after my Mother said call Chandra she does not sound right. I called her and she said to me: "I'm tired; I am just so tired of dealing with this." I immediately Ministered to her and told her keep the faith and how I pray for her total healing all the time. As I pen this short story, I see what has happened. Her prayer was she wanted rest; and my prayer was for total healing and in a unique and unusual way; God answered our prayers. My sister woke up the morning of the 25th of August and played with her two youngest children: Trinitee and Tre and told her husband she could not breathe and he called 911 and while they were enroute he said to her: "You have to get better so that Destinee (Their eldest daughter) will not see you like this." Destinee then walks through the door only to find her Mother on the ground and while Anncee is struggling to breathe she says: "I Want My Daddy; I'm dying!" My niece then says, Daddy; she is not moving or breathing anymore he grabs her and in his arms on their seventh wedding anniversary she draws her last breath… she got her Daddy!

My Sister: The late Mrs. Chandra "Anncee" Ann Lyons-Thornton

November 24, 1979-August 25, 2016

Testimonials of Seasons of Unbearable Grief

Caren Waters

Rowlett, Texas

Sometimes blessings can come in the form of death. Although, the physical is missed, I can feel my mother's presence alive in me. God is absolutely amazing how he can comfort us through what we see an impossible to overcome.

Mrs. LaShonda Runnels

Brookshire Brothers Marketing Category Manager
Lufkin, Texas

When my mother passed in 2012 - I literally felt as though my world and life had been taken from under me. There I was 2 hours away from home as she was taking her final breathes and preparing for her transition. I remember speeding over 100mph and it still felt like I wasn't getting anywhere any faster. I had visited my mother almost every day while she was in the hospital and she looked nothing like herself. But when I finally did make it to her hospital room (after she had already passed) - my mother had this glow that she had never had before. Her skin never seemed purer and her look was of calmness. Because I had to remain strong for my father - I didn't have a chance to grieve for my mother in the beginning. My grieving came days, weeks, months, and years after. I would cry myself to sleep, I battled depression, and truly felt as though life was not going to go on. There were so many unanswered questions that were never asked and so many things that I never got to say. My emotions were all over the place within the first year. It sounds crazy but this was the first time I questioned GOD. Why my mother? And then I thought how selfish of me? There I was questioning the one person who gave his life for me because he decided to relieve my mother of her pain. After many conversations with my pastor - I was able to put all of those questions and unspoken words into a letter. I took this letter to her grave and read each one out loud. In that letter, I asked her questions that only she could answer and I asked for her forgiveness on certain things that transpired early on in life. After I read to her, I screamed, I yelled, and I cried. Finally, my release of GRIEF! In that moment - my mind was clear, my heart was light, and my Faith was restored. Grief is healing, it is about releasing, and there is no rule book to prepare you on how to deal with it. Everyone has their own way of handling it but what is important is that you have to remind yourself that although someone is not here in the physical form does not mean they are no longer in existence - for they are now more alive than they have ever been.

Pastor Cynthia "Cyndi" Doran

Keltys United Methodist Church
Lufkin, Texas

"Good Grief"

When we go through the death of someone special in our lives we think sometimes that nothing good can come from it. However, there is "Good grief" and it is the grief that is used to help reach a higher plateau in life. Ralph Waldo Emerson once spoke to the constellations in the saying that if they came about only every 1,000 years we would find them extraordinary and miraculous! Yet, because they appear in the sky every single night, we hardly acknowledge them at all. Without grief, and acknowledging that grief, we would fail to recognize the quality of life that has taken place. Grief pays homage to that life, if you will, and in doing so allows us to acknowledge how extraordinary and miraculous it was while we shared in it on earth.

It is my belief that in that recognition and acknowledgement through grief we learn to heal from the inside out and that is not done without relying on our Lord and Savior. A tragic death breaks our heart. We are not the creator of the human heart and we do not have the knowledge or means to mend it. It is through our grief that God is enabled to reach deep in our heart where the hurt begins and heal us with his perfect love form the inside out. Nothing that our Heavenly Father does is done half way. When he heals; he does it with a complete effort. If we are not grieving, we are holding back and not opening ourselves up to be healed. Once we allow ourselves to grieve and acknowledge the death; God begins the healing process in us. The healing cannot occur in the heart until the Maker of the heart is able to knit it back together with His perfect love.

The knitting back together of the heart with perfect love allows our heart tune memories that once caused grief into moments of comfort. It also enables us to trust and rely on God. This creates in us a new heart that can grasp the concept of a resurrection and a certainty of our loved one's resurrection. In the book of John, (The eleventh chapter beginning with the twenty-fifth verse) Jesus tells us that He is the resurrection life. He goes on to say, "Those who believe in me, even though they die, yet shall they live, and whoever lives and believes in me shall never die." He closes his thoughts in this passage with, "Because I live, you shall live also." If we have grieved to the extent that we allow Christ in our hearts, then this assurance allows us emotional recovery after our hearts have been mended. Like anything in life, once extra support is added to something; it is strengthened. The assurance that Jesus provides strengthens our faith and in turn makes us a stronger person in life and that is when the grief that started as a horrible state of mind: transforms into the final stage and proves to be one of our greatest blessings.

Once we allow grief to take us to the stages of acknowledgement and allowing God to heal us making us stronger, then we become healing agents ourselves. During these moments it could be stated that our "Good grief" turns into "Great grief" because it is transformed into a gift that can help others. There is no greater feeling than being able to be a voice for Christ in your living out your faith. However, the blessing does not stop there. The seed to this entire process in our lives is the love for a very special person that we have witnessed slip away. Once we arrive at the place where we find strength to share with others in overcoming their grief then we are also sharing a part of our loved one. This sharing of our loved one's life allows that life to go on and continue to be a part of the living here on hearth, even though they now dwell in higher place. There will be a part of your loved one that loves on in your sharing and in your caring for others and none of it would be possible without the grief that acknowledge our seasons of separation. I believe the part that our loved one plays in ministering to others brings Heaven a little closer to earth for us to feel their presence and be assured of their well-being.

Anyone who has suffered a death of a loved one is encouraged to grieve and allow a process to begin. Just like the crucifixion, it starts out a hideous and painful event but when placed in the hands of our Heavenly Father it grows and matures into a blessing that can honor and highlight our Master.

This book was inspired by these experiences:

DOCTOR M.E. LYONS
(In the transition of my Father)

DOCTOR M.E. LYONS
(In the transition of my Sister)

PASTOR CYNTHIA "CYNDI" DORAN
(In the transition of my Father)

MRS. LaSHONDA RUNNELS
(In the transition of her Mother)

MS. DEVIANN DOGGETT
(In the transition of her Mother)

MRS. MICHELE INGRAM
(In the transition of her Mother)

MS. CAREN WATERS
(In the transition of her Mother)

PASTOR CHRISTOPHER MOORE
(In the transition of his Mother)

PASTOR ROY SCOTT
(In the transition of his Mother)

RAY MONTGOMERY, JR.
(In the transition of his Father)

THE O'NEIL FAMILY~ *Dallas, Texas*
*(Ms. Caren O'Neil was a cousin who
succumbed to breast cancer)*

Book Dedication

To my cousin Caren O'Neil who has always been one that was full of life, vigor, and life. This cousin always wore a smile on her face; as least every time I saw her. She recently found out that she had breast cancer and immediately started making arrangements for her two little girls to be taken care and I kept up with her on Facebook and saw the progress that she was making and even posting videos and posts concerning how she would beat this cancer. I knew she would and prayed that she would. We had a connection: herself, her older sister who her and I are the same age: La 'Treshur and their little sister Jenny and one of my younger sisters: Chandra used to spend countless hours together at my cousins Archie and Lois' house. While our parents and their parents played dominos and spades all night long it gave us the opportunity to bond as cousins; and that we did. So when I was attending a friend of mine funeral service in Dallas, Texas and received the text message that they would be removing her from off of life support: my heart dropped. I was thinking: not Caren; she is a fighter and full of life. I and my wife traveled to the hospital and there I walked in and saw her lifeless body and it was surreal. How could someone who was always smiling and full of life be without life? I was asked to preside and deliver the eulogy which was one of the hardest things I have ever done; because it was if I had to speak of my sister and that is exactly how it felt. I dedicate this book to Caren for how she affected my life. I dedicate it to those who struggle with breast cancer and those who have been unwillingly enrolled into the class of being separated from their loved ones through breast cancer and pray that God would yield a remedy, anecdote and cure for this evil that robs so many of us of the potential to see those we love accomplish the feats that we were so desperately waiting to witness. I love you Caren and the world is a lot less funny without you!

A Poem Written, Read and Commemorating the life of Caren O'Neil

"That's Who I Am"

Saturday the 29th in the month of May,
Was the day I received the word I could no longer stay,
My days were spent with the ones who are my fam,
If you want to know Carren; that's who I am.

God blessed me with two little angels
that were my glamour girls,
Gabriel and Abigail they were truly my whole world,
My weeks were spent with the ones who are my fam,
If you want to know Carren; that's who I am.

My favorite thing to say was the phrase "Cool beans,"
If you really know who I am you'll know what it means,
My months were spent with the ones who are my fam,
If you want to know Carren; that's who I am.

I thank God for my parents; Linda and Ocie,
You hold your heads up high; there's no need to worry,
To my sisters; Treshur and Jenny Oh:
I cannot forget Nathan,
You stuck in there through thick and
thin; without any persuasion,
My years were spent with the ones who are my fam,
If you want to know Caren; that's who I am.

To all of you my family and the one whom we share seeds,
After the day is over I hope the message of hope leads,
Each of you into a better place; and feeds all of your needs,
My life was spent with the one who are my fam,
If you want to know where Carren is;
I am in the arms of the Lamb!

GRIEF PRINCIPLE ONE
"It Does Not Happen Overnight"

You cannot get over in five days what has been going on for thirty years! Thirty years multiplied by twelve months and the weeks constitute for a lifetime of grief! Many times those who surround the person(s) who directly affected by grief during their seasons of separation are often coached into believing that after a while when they are unaware of the investment that has placed in the life that is now gone. Say for instance, a couple has married for fifty plus years; it took them fifty plus years to garner the love that they have had for each other that grew over the course of the years and to expect that person to go lay down in the bed that they shared for fifty years, or sit at a breakfast table where they spent countless years communicating, or even do things alone that they have done together for over a half a century is an ambiguity. No one knows the investment that has been made, and thereby can assess the period of getting over it. Perhaps it is not a marriage; it could be a child who never came home and ran the streets, it could be a child who never had a relationship with their parents and something happened to remove them from this walk of life; their parents could react one of two ways. They could react as if, they did not exist before why cry now; or they could grieve over the fact that they never had a relationship over their child and that could be a lifetime or a moment of grief; depending upon how one approaches the circumstance. Grief is something that cannot be made sense of to be very truthful. A mother who has held her child once and then the child drifts way could experience the same grief or even greater grief than the Mother who has watched their child take their first steps, graduate school, go to college, get married, have grandchildren and everything else. We cannot align a time table to grief because we know not when grief will lighten or become heavier.

"Grief is like fingerprints; each has their own identities"
M.E. Lyons

Grief Principle Two

"Grief Is Unique"

Grief may be mingled with resentment, regret, or strife. There is no grief like my grief. The worst grief in the world is the grief that I deal with. This is the testimony for any person; if they be honest. Some people deal with grief much differently than others. There are times within my struggle with grief, whereas I am laughing over reminiscing the days my Father spent together. There were times were there were comical things that happen over the years and it causes me to laugh a little harder because of how much more of an appreciation I have for the memory now than then. But then there are times whereas I could be laughing and think of my Father and tears begin to run down my cheeks and my heart begins to ache and the question now rests upon my lips; why could I not have said something else to him, or did something else for him. Grief can be very bully-ish. It has a way of demanding what you should do when it desires for it to take place. Songs can trigger emotions, smells, certain movies, places and many others can navigate your feelings.

Grief is so unique that no one can actually admit that every death has ever felt the same. The death of a Mother is different from the death of a Father. Just like the death of a sister is different than the death of a brother, and likewise of a child or friend. Every death comes with its own heart strings.

> *"My Grief can never be likened to your grief!"*
> *M.E. Lyons*

GRIEF PRINCIPLE THREE

Grief's Components

This principle is much shorter than the others, but just as if not more important to the grieving process. Grief is comprised of several components, and they are: happiness, loneliness, anger, depression, and resentment. These components are essential to the healing process. If they are expected, then the person dealing with the grief would be able to handle it better with an understanding that grief can come several different ways!

"Grief has more than one face!"
M.E. Lyons

GRIEF PRINCIPLE FOUR

"In Your Own Time"

Do not let anyone in groups or friends or family push you when you are not prepared and ready to talk about it. One thing that much be mentioned concerning grief is the fact that **grief it is pushed; becomes grief that is avoided**. The more a person is pushed to talk about it; the more they harbor and hide from the surface of their mind. They begin to place the grief under the metaphorical rugs of their mind in order to appeal to the overwhelming pressure from those who are around. If we would allow them to talk in their own time it would be more therapeutic! Perhaps they are still in a stage of grief; which we speak about later in this book more in depth. Maybe they are struggling with another stage and our pushing them causes them to skip a stage which only doubles back in the form of a much greater struggle. For instance, a Mother who has a child who has been murdered has laid her child to rest two weeks prior and we were to stop by and try and get her to talk about the incident. She may still be dealing with anger and we try and coach her past the anger before time; she then skips it and later in life she runs across a child who reminds her of her late child and now anger has taken the form of hatred for every child who is around the same age, looks like her child, talks like her child and now she is taken to be a person who does not like children. Grief must be dealt with as it comes and not rushed, nor aborted. Only God can fully remove any hurt that we can ever imagine. Even David when his child that was birthed by Bathsheba died; those who were around him let him be until HE was ready to move on. He sat in ashes and shaved his head and one day out of nowhere he got up and cleaned himself up and asked for some food. His mourning, depressed, and lonely days was over.

"Grief can never be bullied; it must take its course"
M.E. Lyons

GRIEF PRINCIPLE FIVE

"Don't Coach Your Grief"

Grieving is a natural process and moping and constantly having your mind on the incident causes one to not see the purpose of the pain. Go about your day as normal and as grieving arises in your mind and spirit then allow it to happen and not sitting around doing nothing and cultivate a mode of depression. You see beloved, one cannot try and throw a pity party behind grief; because all this does is add more weight to the burden that you are already carrying. When a person coaches a thing, they run plays, watches the players every move, they spend countless hours figuring out way how to make the team win. It is no different with coaching grief; the plays are translated to thoughts, the player's movement is then translated as everything is about the person that has slipped away, and the countless hours figuring out how to win becomes the subconscious way of finding out how to stay where you are. Coaching one's grief will create a deep environment of depression. When my Father had first passed away; it was so bad I could never even say he had died. I always said when he fell asleep; it made me feel better. All of the while I coached my grief; I had good days that were interwoven with several bad hours and moments. It consumed me; I was becoming so inundated and overwhelmed with his dying that my living was placed on the back burner. I developed high blood pressure and my family was suffering because I was always in a bad place. My youngest son then; Jeremiah got to the point whereas he would say to my wife; Daddy is crying about his Daddy again. He then said one day to me that it was alright: Big-Daddy is ok. I then realized, that I could no longer coach my grief, because it was becoming who I was. After all, I preach about death and death is inevitable; how could I be so overwhelmed with something that is the very vehicle to what we hope for? Coaching our grief can cause health issues, depression, disgust, disappointment and even death for us. Do you think that our dying would make things better due to our consumption in the inevitable?

"Grief is like breathing; let it be!"
M.E. Lyons

GRIEF PRINCIPLE SIX

"Grief Is Like A Roller Coaster"

Grief is like a roller coaster; embrace it as it comes. There is simply no way to brace yourself for something that you do not see coming. Even if a loved one is giving a certain amount of time. Most times our minds are not fully wrapped around the fact that they are transitioning to another place. Roller coasters are something that I care not to ever ride. I have ridden the kiddie roller coasters at the State Fair of Texas and that is it, and they even take my breath away. Roller coasters, such as the Texas Giant and Batman, and all of the other whip around, upside down, and 100 miles per hour rides were not created with me in mind for certain. They climb up seemingly thousands of feet in the air, and then as it creeps up the steep climb, it falls even faster, around the corner at alarming rates of speed and then it loops upside down and sometimes hangs there a moment in time and then comes to a squelching halt. That is the true definition of grief. We could close the book right there. I tell those I attempt to Minister to all of the time: "Grief is like a roller coaster." You are level at one moment and then you are at the top of your life the next and then before you know it your stomach is gone and then around the corner you go and then it is over; only to find out the ride has begun again. There is no limit to how many times the roller coaster will take off and finish and then it could happen at the most inopportune time. Ride it with dignity and just embrace and accept the fact that your heart has the control panel and it has no specific limits to how many times you ride it.

"Embrace the inevitable"
M.E. Lyons

GRIEF PRINCIPLE SEVEN

"You Don't Get Over This"

Death is not something you get over; it is something you learn to live with. Several people say upon their learning of your season of separation: you will get over it. This is the biggest lie ever told das it pertains to death. It is something that a person must learn to live with. Because if you could get over it, it would never hurt again. I have never known anyone who has experience death and never hurt about it again. If this was the case; they would not still possess pictures, speak of the person absent, they would never cry about them. We were built to love each other and find a place in our heart to place that person for a lifetime. Think about it; Jesus shows up to the tomb of Lazarus and after all of the drama has been avoided with Martha he stands at the tomb and what does Jesus do? Wept. Not cried, but he wept. Why would Jesus weep and he told us not to weep as those who have no hope? He wept because once you are in a heart; you are always in a heart. You do not get over it; even if you are JESUS!

"Grief is like taxes; there is no getting around it!"

Grief Principle Eight

"You Cannot Avoid This"

Grief is something that will happen no matter how hard you try to avoid it but one you experience it is not a place you stay; you visit there and then allow life to continue while embracing the moments in the years to come. Grief that is nurtured a while turns into depression which after time becomes a life without purpose! It turns into a life without purpose because you no longer to strive and be better and accomplish different ventures in life; you now become enthralled with the fact that you wanted to act as if it never happened. There are different stages of grief: denial, anger, frustration, acceptance, depression, happiness and mood swings. When a person first learns of a death most likely they first experience: denial. They experience more times than not for the simple reason that we often say: you have to be kidding me, this could not have happened, I do not believe it. We spend much time trying to figure out why this should not be than we do accepting the fact that it did. Once we accept the death the next stage could be any of them because they happen according to the relationship we have with the loved one. Frustration normally follows denial because then you have no explanation of the why. After frustration has finished usually there is acceptance and with acceptance brings about depression, happiness and mood swings.

You see, when dealing with our seasons of separation our knowing that we cannot avoid this thing called grief enables us to be empowered by knowing the road we have to travel.

"Grief is like running from our shadow; it cannot be outrun!"
M.E. Lyons

GRIEF PRINCIPLE NINE

"Don't Be Afraid To Cry"

Every time I am afforded to officiate or eulogize during a memorial service; I make it known without any equivocations that you should feel free to cry. God created us with tear ducts and they are there for that reason. We hurt as humans and crying cleanses us. Crying releases pressure and pain. If we do not cry it causes health issues: strokes, heart attacks, high blood pressure, and even cancer. Stress causes cancer; and it has been displayed through much research. Holding it in weakens our immune system and cause us to become sick. Whereas, releasing it through a cry, scream or just letting it out makes us become a lot less prone to losing our mind or becoming mental attempting to be some super saint or Christian. No person should fall victim to that age old saying for those who are looked at as being family leaders: "I have to be strong for my family." That cliché is a definite and sure way to end up sick or mental down the line. You miss the opportunity to grieve when necessary and abort the one opportunity to do as everyone needs to do; let it out! I often follow my conviction as well as my training as a funeral director. I attended a mortuary school in Dallas, Texas for funeral directing and embalming and my family has several funeral homes in the DFW metroplex area and one thing I have always tried to do; give the grieving family ample opportunity to do just that: grieve! The funeral home can never rush the family in my presence; for one because this family has paid for this service, two this is the last time on this side that they will see visually their loved ones and there are no do-overs at a funeral. This is why I share with the family to cry. Get it out, because this is it. You will not have this chance again. Do not be afraid to cry.

"Grief is lightened when you cry!"
M.E. Lyons

GRIEF PRINCIPLE TEN

"Accept It"

There is nothing worse in life than walking around with the knowledge of knowing that someone has died and acting as if it has not happened! Not accepting the fact that the person has left here compounds the grief and forces upon us a façade that becomes much more difficult to uphold and even greater to act the part in a play that does not even exist. To play as if nothing has happened is like attempting to hold your breath; it works, but only until you cannot breathe. After you cannot breathe, that which you were trying to hold in; forces its way out and then you are out of breath and now recuperating. The best way to handle grief in a nutshell is to accept it and allow it to take its course. I really hope this book has enabled you to embrace the life left and not to have left life!

"Grief becomes much easier, when we accept it as it is!"
M.E. Lyons

About the Author

Doctor M. E. Lyons has felt the calling of God on his life from his youth and was called into the gospel ministry in 1980 at the tender age of four. Doctor M. E. Lyons is married to the beautiful Latish Luckey-Lyons, and they have four wonderful children: Deja Lyons, Myron E. Lyons II, Jeremiah M. E. Lyons, and Benjamin M. E. Lyons.

He has authored nine books entitled Fresh Air Volume One, The Mind: The Pulpit of God, The Testimony of the Sheep: According to Psalms 23 (a weekly devotional guide), 52 Weeks of Grace: Edition One, Sermons and Illustrations by M. E. First Series, Fresh Air Volume Two, Lessons and Lectures to Live By, A Guide to Grieving, and Smile . . . It Becomes You. Currently, there are seven other books in the process of being published, ranging from second volumes and books concerning marriage/relationships, an autobiography, and a novel on the contrasts of men and women. He has written several songs, poems, and stage plays, and he has also starred in the hit stage play STAT with national recording artist Don Diego. There's a CD (single) featuring Doctor Lyons that has been recently released.

He has attended D. Edwin Johnson Baptist Institute (a seminary) in pastoral studies, evangelism, New Testament survey, Old Testament survey, and southern Baptist heritage. The late Doctor Hardin L. Ward was the instructor. He has attended Dallas Institute of Funeral Services in pursuit of an associate degree in applied sciences in 2005. He underwent music theory with Bernice Abrams in Dallas, Texas. He has also obtained a bachelor of science degree in psychology in applied behavioral analysis from Kaplan University, Davenport, Iowa. He has obtained a master of arts degree in theological studies with emphasis on apologetics and philosophy in Lynchburg, Virginia, from Liberty University. He has obtained a master of arts degree in religious education from Liberty University in Lynchburg, Virginia. He has also received a master of divinity in theology from Liberty University. He has also received a doctorate in divinity from Saint Thomas Christian University in Jacksonville, Florida.

In 2011, he received the necessary invitation from Dr. Joel Gregory to attend Oxford University in London, England, and received certification in homiletics and hermeneutics. He obtained the necessary requirements to become a distinguished gentleman of Oxford. While there, he preached at the Cote Church in the UK.

Printed in the United States
By Bookmasters